Showdow
in the Desert

The Official Book of
Super Bowl XXX

Showdown in the Desert

The Official Book of
Super Bowl XXX

WOODFORD PRESS

SAN FRANCISCO

Creative Director: Laurence J. Hyman
Book Design: Jim Santore
Photography Editor: Dennis Desprois

PHOTOGRAPHERS
Tony Bennett
John E. Biever
Peter Brouillet
Dave Cross
Dennis Desprois
Malcolm W. Emmons
Gerald Gallegos
Beth Hansen
Ross Lewis
David Lilienstein
Al Messerschmidt
Mike Moore
Joe Patronite
Dick Raphael
Bob Rosato
G. B. Rose
Manny Rubio
Paul Spinelli
Kevin Terrell
Tony Tomsic
Ron Vesely
Baron Wolman
Michael Zagaris

The following photographers are from
the Pittsburgh Post-Gazette:
John Beale
Peter Diana
Bob Donaldson
Robin Rombach
Darrell Sapp
Bill Wade

WRITERS
Mark Kreidler
Ed Bouchette
Rob Kelly

CONTENTS

WOODFORD PRESS
660 Market Street
San Francisco, California 94104

ISSN: 1087-0679

ISBN: 0-942627-26-1

First Printing: March 1996
PRINTED AND BOUND IN THE UNITED STATES OF AMERICA
DISTRIBUTED TO THE TRADE BY NATIONAL BOOK
NETWORK, INC.

A History of
Excellence

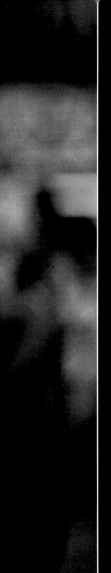

By Ed Bouchette
Pittsburgh Post-Gazette Sports Writer

Dallas vs. Pittsburgh? Fur coats vs. hard hats. Martini & Rossi vs. Iron City beer. The Dallas Cowboys Cheerleaders vs. the Terrible Towels. It's not so much a rivalry as it is culture clash. In fact, about the only thing Pittsburgh and Dallas have in common is football and the passion each city possesses for the game.

The Cowboys and Steelers have met a mere 27 times, including Super Bowl XXX, since the Dallas franchise was born in 1960, and only 11 times since the 1970 NFL merger. That's not exactly the stuff from which rivalries are forged. But when it comes to Super Bowls, Pittsburgh-Dallas is the ultimate rivalry.

The Steelers and Cowboys have met three times in the Super Bowl, more than any other two teams in the NFL. And no others have been able to stage the consistent excitement in the big show that Pittsburgh and Dallas have produced in their three memorable meetings. None of the three games was decided until the final minutes or seconds:

—In Super Bowl X, the Steelers won 21-17 when safety Glen Edwards intercepted Dallas quarterback Roger Staubach's pass in the end zone on the final play.

—In Super Bowl XIII, the Steelers won 35-31 when running back Rocky Bleier recovered the Cowboys' onside kick with 22 seconds left.

—And in Super Bowl XXX, the Steelers trailed by three when the Cowboys' Larry Brown intercepted a Neil O'Donnell pass with just over four minutes left to set up a touchdown in Dallas' 27-17 victory.

And this storied rivalry has showcased some of the biggest

names in the game, names like Staubach, Swann, Harris, Bradshaw, Pearson et al.

After that second meeting, Bleier echoed the feelings of football fans everywhere, "I think the Steelers and the Cowboys have played the two most exciting games ever to be played in the Super Bowl."

You can argue that it is now up to three.

Their games also have helped decide the dominant teams of two different decades. The Steelers' two victories over Dallas helped stamp them as the Team of the 1970s, while the Cowboys' victory over the Steelers in Super Bowl XXX—their third championship of the decade—puts them well on the way to becoming the Team of the 1990s.

"Now I told you I don't care anything about history," Dallas guard Nate Newton said after the Cowboys won their third Super Bowl in four years. "But this three in four years, we're looking at a possible what? Hey, it's a 'D' word."

Dynasty. The Steelers had it in the 1970s: now it's the Cowboys' turn.

This wonderful January rivalry began 20 years ago in Miami, when Dallas and Pittsburgh first met on January 18, 1976, in

Tom Landry

Rocky Bleier

Super Bowl X. The Steelers were defending champs—having beaten Minnesota 16-6 for their first crown in Super Bowl IX— and they were confident they could repeat that feat the next year. "That 1975 team was our best ever," said tackle "Mean" Joe Greene, who missed half the season with nerve damage in his shoulder. "They didn't even need me. The easiest of them all was that second time. We knew from day one where we were going."

Dallas' road to Miami was less smooth. Having failed to make the playoffs the previous season—their first post-season absence in nine years—the Cowboys posted a 10-4 record. But they made the big game only after a Hail Mary pass from Roger Staubach to Drew Pearson with 24 seconds left gave them a 17-14 win over Minnesota in the divisional playoffs.

In Super Bowl X, Dallas took a quick lead on Staubach's 29-yard strike to Pearson. The Steelers evened things up on the next series when they drove 67 yards in 8 plays—one of these plays was a spectacular 32-yard completion to Lynn Swann. Bradshaw capped the drive with a 7-yard scoring strike to tight end Randy Grossman.

A Toni Fritsch field goal gave Dallas a 10-7 halftime lead, and

Chuck Noll and Jimmy Allen

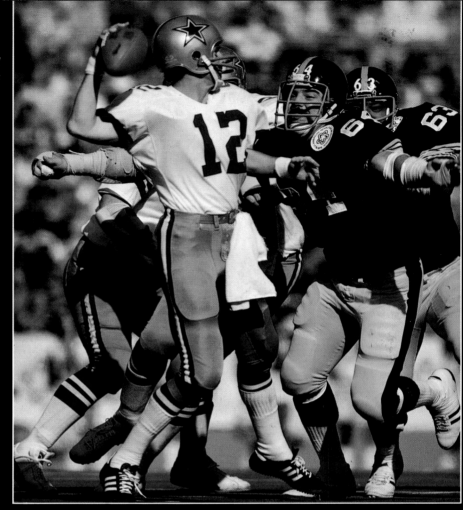

Roger Staubach and Steve Furness

Franco Harris

that mark stood entering the final quarter. Reggie Harrison of Pittsburgh then blocked a Dallas punt that bounced through the end zone for a safety that made it 10-9.

The Steelers got the free kick and drove for Roy Gerela's 36-yard field goal to give them a 12-10 lead. He kicked another from 18 yards for a 15-10 Pittsburgh lead.

What followed was one of the most dramatic plays in Super Bowl history. With three minutes left, quarterback Terry Bradshaw unloaded a deep pass aimed towards Swann. Bradshaw was knocked unconscious by defensive tackle Larry Cole as he released the ball. Swann, who had spent two days in the hospital after suffering a concussion in the AFC Championship Game, caught the ball in stride at the 5-yard line for a 64-yard touchdown that put the Steelers in front 21-10. Despite a late Cowboys touchdown, the Steelers hung on for their second straight Super Bowl victory.

Swann caught four passes for 161 yards and was named the game's MVP.

Drew Pearson

Jackie Smith

"What they were, basically, were great catches," Dallas cornerback Mark Washington said of Swann's circus grabs that day, which included a 53-yard falling-down catch of a tipped ball at midfield that forever will be seen on highlight films.

Dallas got its chance at revenge three years later, on Jan. 21, 1979, again in Miami's Orange Bowl. Dallas was confident entering the contest.

"I think it will be a defensive struggle, but we will prevail," predicted Dallas linebacker Hollywood Henderson.

He was wrong on both counts. The Steelers won 35-31 in a game that was as spectacular as their first meeting.

The first half was an aerial blitz. Terry Bradshaw threw three touchdown passes—28 and 75 yards to John Stallworth, and 7 yards to Rocky Bleier—and Roger Staubach threw one of his own, a 39-yarder to Tony Hill. Dallas' other score came when linebacker Mike Hegman returned a Bradshaw fumble 37 yards for a touchdown. The Steelers were up 21-14 at the half, and that score stood until late in the third quarter.

Dallas moved the ball to the Steelers' 10, where they faced a third down. Staubach found Jackie Smith alone in the end zone. The tight end, known for his sure hands, dropped the perfectly thrown ball and the Cowboys had to settle for a 27-yard Rafael Septien field goal. While Septien's kick made the score 21-17, Dallas never fully recovered.

"I was wide open and I just missed it," said a distraught Smith. "I've dropped passes before, but never one that important."

The Steelers then opened a 35-17 lead on fourth-quarter touchdowns by Franco Harris and Swann, and it seemed that the rout was on with 6:51 left. But someone forgot to give that script to Dallas.

First Staubach threw a 7-yard touchdown pass to Billy Joe DuPree with 2:27 to go. Then Dallas cornerback Dennis Thurman recovered an onside kick and Staubach eventually

John Stallworth

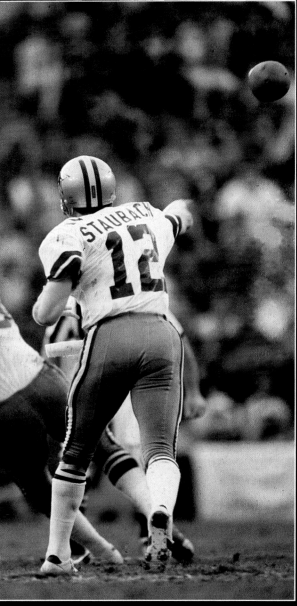

Roger Staubach

pitched a 4-yard touchdown pass to Butch Johnson with 22 seconds left to cut Pittsburgh's lead to four. But any dreams of a miracle comeback were squelched when Bleier recovered the next onside kick try to save the game for the Steelers, who became the first team to win three Super Bowls.

"This is the best football team I've ever seen," Pittsburgh linebacker Jack Ham said afterward.

It would be another 17 years before the teams would meet again in the Super Bowl, and the circumstances would be much different. In the meantime, the NFC had turned the tables on the AFC and dominated the game with 11 straight victories. Dallas was heavily favored to make it an even dozen.

But like all great rivalries, both teams were up to the challenge, and Super Bowl XXX turned into a tense, hard-fought struggle that further etched these two teams' names in the annals of Super Bowl history.

That the game was close should have been no surprise to anybody. More than any other two teams in the NFL, the Cowboys and the Steelers have had a history of great games when a World Championship is on the line. Super Bowl XXX was just another in a trio of heart-stopping battles that kept fans on the edge of their seats to the very end. In a game that has too often featured blowouts, Super Bowl XXX—like X and XIII—lived up to its name. xxx

Jack Lambert

Welcome to the Valley of the Sun

"Hey, can I have your autograph? Who are you?"

—*Signature seeker at
the NFL Experience*

"I think everybody was kind of pretty cool until we got off the plane. When I saw all of those Steelers fans I was amazed. I never expected that."

—*Ray Seals, Pittsburgh*

Steelers Owner Dan Rooney and the team are greeted at Phoenix Airport by their fans.

"It was just awesome out there: the grass was greener than I've ever seen it and the ball was nice and brown and the lights were brighter than I've ever seen. That's the Super Bowl, that's what it's all about."

—*Scott Case, Dallas*

Left, Pittsburgh's Greg Lloyd (white hat) and Rod Woodson hit the ground in Phoenix. Below, Kevin Greene gets his first taste of Super Bowl fever. Opposite, Dallas' Deion Sanders relaxes with the team.

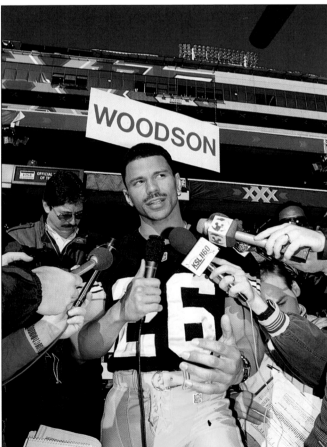

The media day circus rolls into Tempe, with the Cowboys and Steelers posing for their team pictures and, left to right, Rod Woodson, Barry Switzer and Jerry Jones, and Kordell Stewart taking their turns in the spotlight.

"To me, every time we've been here, it's been sweeter and sweeter. Every time we've come back, it's been harder, and that's what makes it much more enjoyable."
—*Jay Novacek, Dallas*

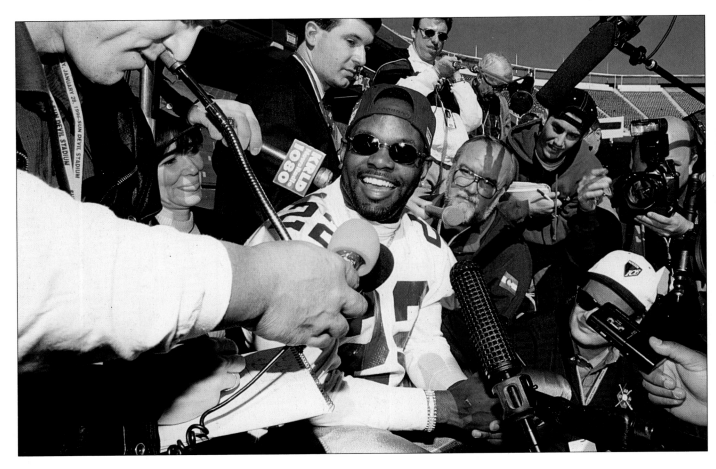

"I was never a Cowboys fan. I was the type of kid growing up who cheered for any team the Cowboys were playing. I just couldn't stand the Cowboys, and Pittsburgh was a big rival at that time. They were the best team in the league and that's who I rooted for."

—*Darren Woodson,
Dallas*

Clockwise from top left, Emmitt Smith, Bill Cowher and Neil O'Donnell speak with the media throng; Bill Bates (left) and Charles Haley goof around; Charles Johnson (left) with Jason Gildon.

"Most people get upset when they have balls thrown at them. I look at it as an opportunity."
—Larry Brown, Dallas

Below, Troy Aikman is the center of attention. Above, Greg Lloyd and right, his teammates, used to the cool weather in Pittsburgh, enjoy the warmth of the desert sun.

The Steelers hang out. Posing and pontificating are Barry, Jerry, Troy and Emmitt.

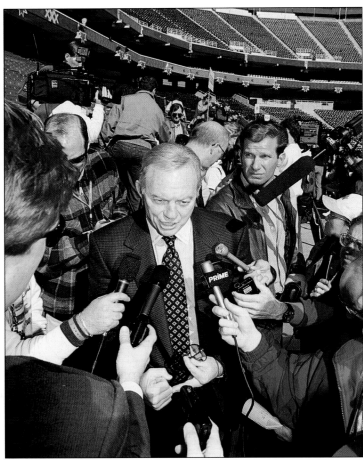

"The whole thing is to really get in there and stop Emmitt Smith. That's who they want to give the ball to. It's no secret there."

—*Greg Lloyd, Pittsburgh*

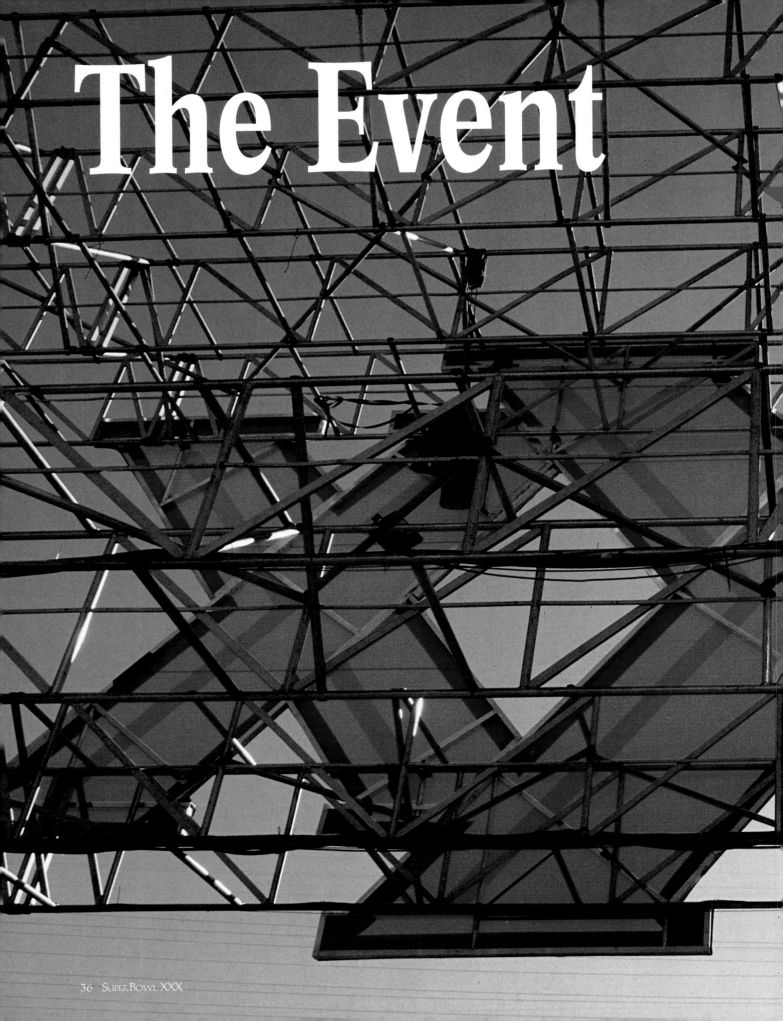

The Event

The NFL Experience, which is an interactive theme park for kids and families, gives fans a chance to test their football skills, get autographs and generally have a good time. The NFL Super Bowl XXX Youth Clinics (below) featured more than 50 current NFL players teaching kids fundamentals of the game.

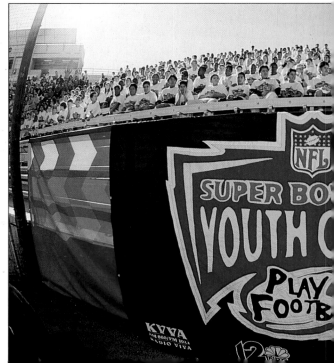

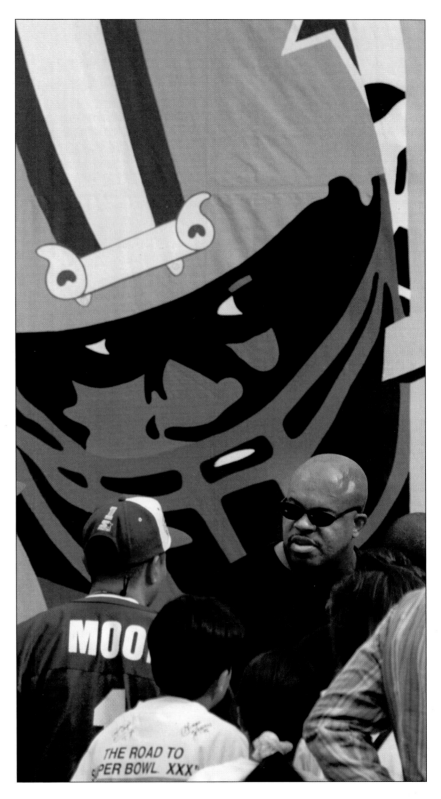

"This is amazing! I don't even have a ticket, and this is still the best time I've ever had."
—*Phil Bellows, Kansas City, Kan.*

The Parada del Sol Super Bowl XXX Parade in Scottsdale featured face painting, cowboys of the old west, smiling faces and even a mobile cactus.

NFL Commissioner Paul Tagliabue, top right, led NFL players and celebrities in Christmas in April, USA "Kickoff to Rebuild '96," the nation's largest volunteer home rehabilitation initiative. This group helped rebuild two homes close to Sun Devil Stadium.

"It shows my age. They ask me what Super Bowl I played in, and when you say XIII and they're on XXX now, it seems like light years away."

> —*Former Dallas receiver Tony Hill, who played in the Cowboys' 35-31 loss to Pittsburgh in Super Bowl XIII.*

Arizona Cardinals Owner Bill Bidwill autographs a football for a fan at the groundbreaking ceremony for the NFL's Youth Education Town.

"We're here and the Super Bowl is taking place. The crowd at the airport. We have security. We have Super Bowl packets. It's finally here. It's getting exciting now."
—*Norm Johnson, Pittsburgh*

Young fans dive, bounce and gaze in wonder at The NFL Experience.

"WOW!"
—*Young fan
at The NFL
Experience*

Going all out is not a trait reserved only for players. At The NFL Experience, everyone gets a chance to test his or her skills—or lack thereof.

"Pant, gasp, cough, hack!"

—*Older fan running 50-yard dash at The NFL Experience*

Sand sculptures in a Phoenix mall capture the spirit of the Super Bowl.

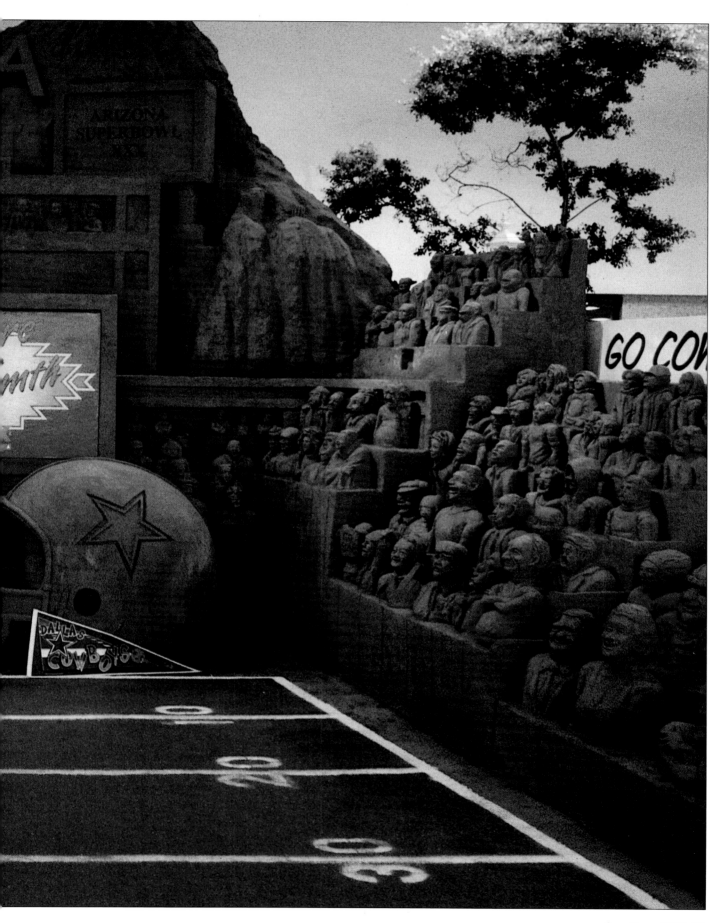

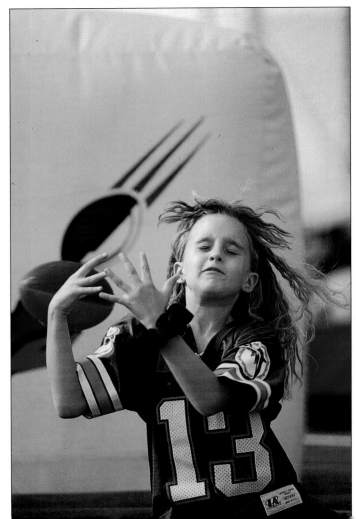

"I think the important thing is for everyone to enjoy themselves and have fun this week. This football team has earned that right and deserves it. But also we've got to keep in mind why we're here."

—*Troy Aikman, Dallas*

"If Art Monk can still play in the NFL, then maybe somebody will notice me. I can make a comeback."

> *—Ex-Cowboys receiver Drew Pearson, warming up for the NFL Throwbacks Bowl, a flag football game featuring 20 retired league legends.*

Children have a great time during Super Bowl week, whether they are getting tips at a Youth Clinic, securing an autograph, playing around with a helmet or posing for a picture.

Below, Bill Cowher during interview number 256 for the week. Right top, the MVP Luncheon featured, left to right, Franco Harris, Paul Tagliabue and Roger Staubach. Jay Leno and The Tonight Show, right below, were in town for the festivities.

"If you're a football fan, this is the center of the universe."

—*Steve Ambrose, Dallas fan*

"Winning is the epitome of honesty itself."
—*Woody Hayes, 1977.*

By Mark Kreidler

There are no second acts, only secondary actors. There is no amount of chatter—esoterica, hyperbole, fish-tales or outright grandaddy lies—that could ever overwhelm the essential element of accomplishment. As a wise man (who may or may not have worn shoulder pads) once said, "It ain't braggin' if you can back it up."

Woody Hayes never made the sideline of a Super Bowl, and he surely never got a load of these Dallas Cowboys. But Hayes had it right, in the end: When they hand you the trophy, that is the Truth.

The rest? It's all just talk.

The thirtieth anniversary of what has become the biggest spectacle in sports had a chance, for nearly a week there, to become better remembered for what happened near the field than for what happened on it. It had such a chance because the Dallas Cowboys are world-class talkers; and because talk, around Super Bowl time, is just remarkably cheap; and because there is nothing quite so embraceable in the world of sports as the Big Buildup to the Big Event. The Cowboys build it up like nobody's business. Build it up? Listen, they layer it, one giant mound at a time.

And so there they were, in the week preceding Super Bowl XXX, treating the Arizona area and their temporary digs in Tempe as a full-on home away from home. It was the Cowboys who threw the parties, the Cowboys who arrived in the limousines, the Cowboys who created the controversies and the bulletin-board one-liners and the Cowboys who clutched the entire proceeding to their collective chest like nothing so much as an old friend. If you came in late, you would have been forgiven a little confusion: Dallas wasn't the host of this game; it just behaved like it.

And this is what could have been taken from Super Bowl

Battle For Greatness

XXX, the Large Yak. But then they played. The Cowboys and the Pittsburgh Steelers played football, and what transpired on the floor of Sun Devil Stadium, a 27-17 Dallas victory that seemed ever so uncertain until the waning moments of a long, desperately beautiful Arizona evening, was enough to remind you that, at the finish, the play's the thing.

This was, beyond its unprecedented flash, a Super Bowl of tremendous dimension, buoyed by the history between the teams—their past meetings in Super Bowls X and XIII, the epic Noll-Landry and Bradshaw-Staubach battles—and by Dallas' own attempt to create a new kind of history with its third Lombardi Trophy in four years. In an age of runaway free agency and the egalitarian effects of the salary cap, such an achievement clearly would place the Cowboys among the elite teams of the modern years. As the Steelers had dominated the 1970s, and the San Francisco 49ers were regarded as the team of the 1980s, so did Dallas Owner Jerry

Jones want his team to be recognized as the best in this decade.

And so it would be—but not without a struggle. It was a struggle that surprised the majority, who, surveying the previous 11 years of American Football Conference futility in this game, mistook the Steelers for a Super patsy. And it was a struggle that, in so many significant ways, mirrored the Season That Was, deep in the heart of Texas.

That the Cowboys should arrive in Phoenix with their swagger intact was a minor curiosity in its own right; the truth was, this had been a year of deep soul searching among the members of the team and their fans, many of whom still hadn't recovered from a jolting 38-28 defeat by the 49ers in the NFC Championship Game the season before.

That loss, coming after two straight Jimmy Johnson-led victories over San Francisco in previous title matches, came in the Cowboys' first season under Barry Switzer. And by the time Switzer and his staff began gearing up for another

By the time the Cowboys reached Phoenix, it still was almost impossible to tell whether any of the expectations had been met. Yes, Dallas was back in the Super Bowl; but had a 12-4 regular-season record ever felt shakier? The Cowboys had lost twice to lowly Washington, been soundly beaten at home by the 49ers and tasted defeat in Philadelphia after two crucial failures on fourth-and-one deep in their own territory (the first was nullified by the two-minute warning) handed the Eagles a game-winning field goal.

It was, in many respects, a film negative of the road to the Super Bowl taken by the Steelers, who turned in a late-season eight-game winning streak. For Pittsburgh and fourth-year Head Coach Bill Cowher, this was a season of the sweetest redemption. Like the Cowboys, the Steelers had suffered a difficult defeat in their conference championship the year before, a 17-13 shocker by the San Diego Chargers. Like the Cowboys, the Steelers had carried the memory of the game with them through the 1995 season.

The difference? Essentially, it was perspective. Whereas Dallas' inability to reach the Super Bowl in 1994 had been taken as evidence of a worrisome decline, Cowher, his players and their followers seemed to recognize that Pittsburgh's appearance in the 1994 AFC Championship Game was perhaps a harbinger of good times to come. And they were right: A year later, against the Indianapolis Colts, the Steelers' second straight title game came down to a pulsating final minute of play. But whereas Neil O'Donnell's fourth-down pass was batted away to seal the Steelers' defeat

run in 1995, the number of losses from the Johnson era had reached staggering proportions: linebacker Ken Norton Jr., wide receiver Alvin Harper, safeties James Washington and Thomas Everett, defensive end Jim Jeffcoat, guards Kevin Gogan and John Gesek, defensive tackles Jimmie Jones and Tony Casillas, center Mark Stepnoski. Ten former full-time or part-time starters gone—and, too, four of Johnson's top assistant coaches: Norv Turner, Dave Wannstedt, Tony Wise and Butch Davis.

What was left? A very good team, but not necessarily a dynastic one. There were Troy Aikman, Michael Irvin and Emmitt Smith. There were some of the best offensive linemen in the business. There were adequate and occasionally brilliant defenders—Charles Haley, Leon Lett, Darren Woodson, the recently signed Deion Sanders.

And there were expectations. And they were not going away.

Said Switzer, "I told my children after [owner] Jerry Jones offered me the job, 'It's not going to be a cakewalk. We are fixing to go through some tough times. It's something that's going to be difficult for you to handle.' I arrived here with the expectations of going to the Super Bowl and winning the Super Bowl. I know when Jimmy arrived here at 1-15 [the record in Johnson's first season as head coach], there wasn't that expectation."

by the Chargers, this time it was a Hail-Mary pass thrown by the Colts' Jim Harbaugh that somehow bounced loose and fell to the ground, concluding a 20-16 Pittsburgh victory and one of the most thrilling championship finishes in recent memory. The Steelers, with Cowher just 38 years old, had reached the Super Bowl for the first time since 1979.

This was a year in which Cowher and his staff made critical adjustments to a team already perceived as strong enough to take the AFC. With leading rusher Barry Foster gone, the Steelers went to a tandem running game of Erric Pegram and Bam Morris and, more importantly, opened up their passing attack, often employing five wide receivers at once. In Colorado rookie Kordell Stewart, Cowher and his staff crafted a player so versatile that his nickname became "Slash," as in, quarterback-slash-running back-slash-wide receiver. Stewart quickly emerged as one of the most dangerous and unpredictable players in the league—and Cowher had himself a hit.

"Bill Cowher has brought an aggressive style to this team," said Steelers cornerback Carnell Lake. "He's been able to manipulate his talent and utilize it where some teams wouldn't do it, like with Kordell. Who would take a quarterback that they drafted in the second round and use

him the way they use him? He throws, he runs, he punts the ball. You have to have some kind of aggressiveness to do that, and I think players feed off that."

Indeed, Cowher was nothing if not confident; and, in players like linebackers Greg Lloyd and Kevin Greene, he fashioned a team that played that way. But, as Pittsburgh was to learn, nobody does confidence like the Dallas Cowboys of the 1990s.

The Cowboys were installed as huge favorites for Super Bowl XXX, their well-chronicled concerns notwithstanding; and they hit Phoenix with no indication that they felt things should be otherwise. The week before the game was filled with anecdotes that ranged from amusing to preposterous: Dallas players arriving at practice in stretch limousines; spending late nights on the town; claiming a "home-field advantage" at Sun Devil Stadium because they had played there so often and had a large local following in the Phoenix area.

Aikman nearly blanched at some of the histrionics, perhaps fearing a strong Pittsburgh reaction. Switzer feigned indifference. But it was Irvin who came closest to the truth when he said, "I am not worried about giving anyone extra juice here. I don't think that at this point—playing in the

Super Bowl, playing for what's at stake—there is any such thing as giving you extra juice . . . Being here is part of the reward. The rest of the reward is winning it."

As it developed, and despite the occasional appearance during Super Bowl week, the Cowboys already had passed their moment of crisis. And, oddly enough, it was the Philadelphia game, with its fateful fourth-down calls by Switzer, that the players said helped them turn an important corner.

"The whole team wanted to go for it," safety Bill Bates said of Switzer's decisions against the Eagles. "When we didn't make it, and coach Switzer took all the heat for making the calls, we said, 'Hey, forget what everybody else says. Let's rally. We are family, and let's stay together and let

it fly the last part of the season.' And we did."

Dallas had finished its schedule with a shaky victory over the Giants and a solid one over the Cardinals, then disposed of the Eagles and Packers in the playoffs. The Cowboys were healthy, with their chance at history as the ultimate motivator. And, in the end, they neither overpowered nor overwhelmed the Steelers, but instead logged a performance that matched almost precisely the tenor of their season: They did just enough.

In fact, Super Bowl XXX would turn on two plays, both of which were more memorable for what Pittsburgh failed to do than for anything that Dallas did—two interceptions thrown by O'Donnell, both in the second half, both leading to Dallas touchdowns, the final one icing a tremendously close game.

It was a struggle, every bit of it. Under a perfect, clear desert sky, the Cowboys squeezed 13 points out of their first three possessions; but buried under the numbers was the fact that, despite controlling the flow and tempo of the game, Dallas had been able to convert only one of three TD opportunities, settling for Chris Boniol field goals on the other two. The Steelers were locked in a grim, bend-but-don't-break fight, and yet when O'Donnell hit Yancey Thigpen with a six-yard scoring pass just before halftime, two quarters of getting pushed around had left them behind by only 13-7.

This set the stage for a second half that Pittsburgh managed to command without ever seizing. The Steelers held the ball for more than 21 of the half's 30 minutes; they piled up 201 yards of offense; they tried an onside kick while trailing 20-10 early in the fourth quarter and made it work, marching in for the touchdown that made it 20-17. It was Pittsburgh in a walkover.

Except, of course, that it wasn't. For while the Cowboys allowed the battle's control to swing to the other side, they never made the killing mistake that would lose them the war. O'Donnell, whose consistency was a hallmark of Pittsburgh's season, did.

On the Steelers' second possession of the half, his team trailing 13-7, O'Donnell looked to pass upfield. But the ball slipped from his hand and floated directly to Dallas cornerback Larry Brown, who returned it 44 yards to set up a touchdown run by Smith.

"It just got away from me," O'Donnell said. "Those things happen."

What happened the second time was less easily explained, and ultimately critical. With the score 20-17, barely four minutes left to play and the Steelers having just forced a Dallas punt, O'Donnell took a snap out of the shotgun and aimed a pass to the right side . . . where, once again, the Cowboys' Brown was the only player near it. Wide receiver Andre Hastings had broken inside—the play was designed to go either inside or outside—but O'Donnell threw outside. Brown, who would be voted the game's Most Valuable Player, had an open lane up the field and returned his second interception 33 yards to the Pittsburgh 6. Two plays later, Smith plunged across with the game's final score.

"I just thank God," said Brown, who had endured a season which included the death of his prematurely-born son, plus the intense heat of being the cornerback playing opposite the brilliant Sanders. "I'm happy for Coach Switzer and I'm glad to play for the best organization in professional football, the Dallas Cowboys."

At the finish, the Cowboys did find their history. They shook off the ghost of 1995's disappointment, played through

what Emmitt Smith called "a lot of adversity, trials and tribulations," and departed Super Bowl XXX with their third championship ring in four seasons. They did not dominate the Pittsburgh Steelers, not by any measure. They rattled. They rolled. At times, they smoked and sputtered. But when the air cleared, NFL Commissioner Paul Tagliabue was handing the Lombardi Trophy to beaming Jerry Jones.

"We did it our way, baby!" Barry Switzer screamed to Jones, just after the final seconds clicked off the Sun Devil Stadium scoreboard. In just about every way—the talk, the walk and the result—Switzer got it exactly right.

Pregame

People show their true colors on Super Bowl Sunday, whether in the hats they wear, the patches on their shirts or the colors of their costumes.

"Any game—not just the Super Bowl—if you lose the turnover battle, you can't win the game."
—*Rod Woodson, Pittsburgh*

"People don't have a clue what life is going to be like around here. People have already made up their minds that this is their reward. It's just a party. People don't care. They throw all reason out the window."

—Ex-Cowboys quarterback Danny White, warning Phoenix residents of the Super Bowl tsunami of eats, drinks and festivities a few days before it arrived.

As game time approaches, everyone—the fans in the stands, party goers, the game's broadcasters and enormous poultry—is ready for kickoff.

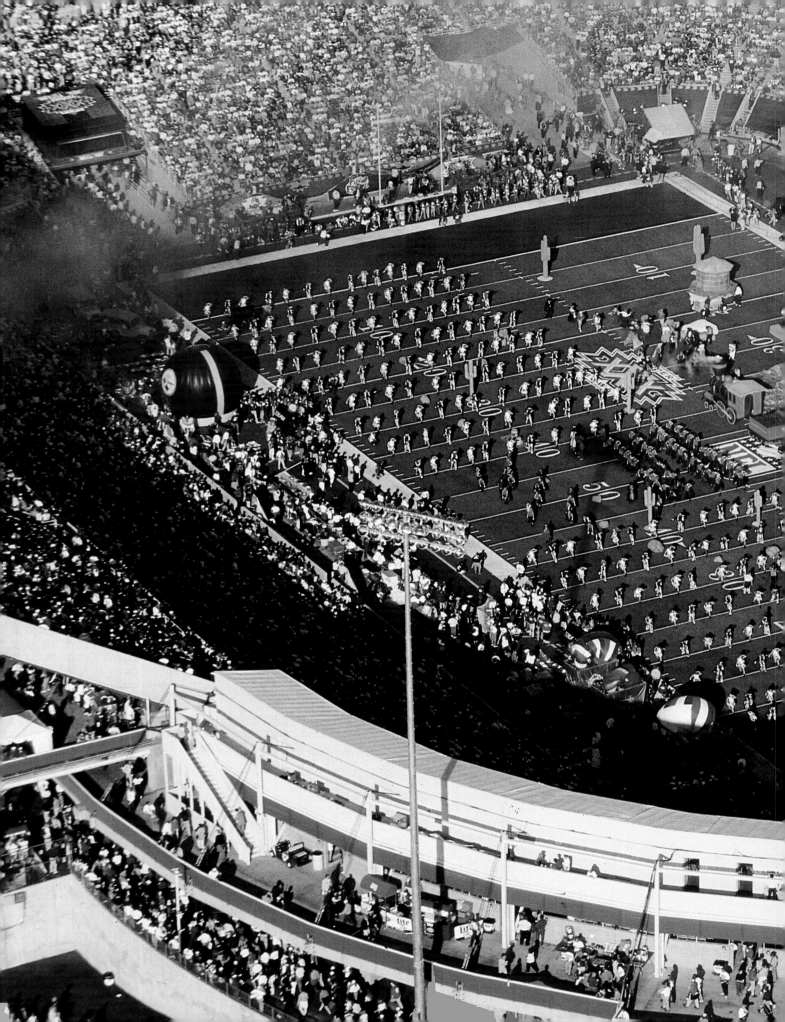

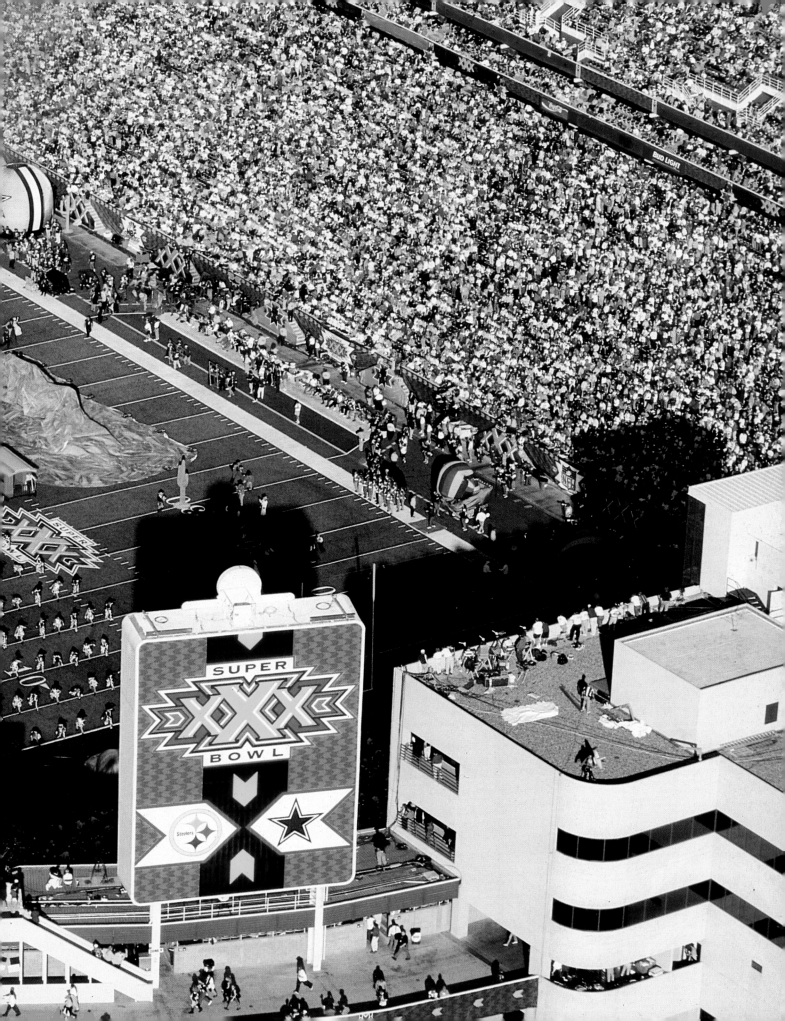

"For the Steelers to win, they have to play a flawless game . . . Dallas has the luxury that they don't have to play flawlessly. They can make mistakes. They have a lot of weapons. I would have to go with Dallas."

—Rocky Bleier, running back on all four Pittsburgh Super Bowl championship teams.

"As soon as this game ends, whether we win or lose, it starts all over again. Nobody really cares about the fact that we won the Super Bowl. It's what are you going to do to try to do it again next year. It's a vicious cycle."
    —*Troy Aikman, Dallas*

With minutes to go before kickoff, the field is adorned in color, from Native Americans of the Southwest to cowboys . . . some of whom stage a shootout in a pre-game stunt show.

"Personally, I don't get caught up in being the underdog. I think they're looking at it like that because Dallas has been here a couple of times. We're new to it."
—*Neil O'Donnell, Pittsburgh*

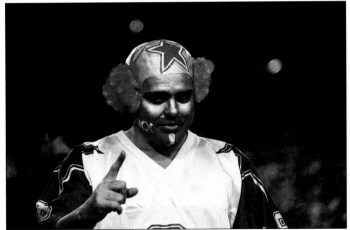

"All the talking doesn't win games. Deeds do. We feel confident on where we are and how we got here. Other people can talk about it. We're going to go out and do it."
—*Bill Cowher, Pittsburgh*

"I want to see them come out of the shadow of the Steelers of the 1970s. A great career is nice, but all people remember is winning."

—*Ex-Steelers
cornerback Mel Blount*

Meet the gladiators: Troy Aikman, Michael Irvin and Derek Kennard are introduced with the rest of the Dallas offense.

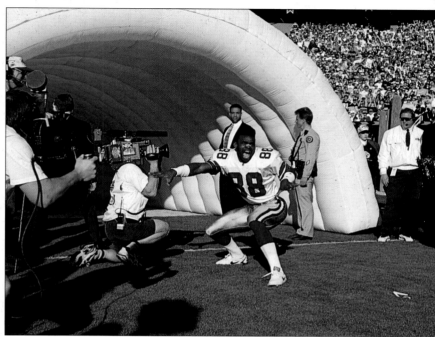

"I would like to think that if we're clicking, nobody can stop us."
—Michael Irvin, Dallas

Ray Seals takes to the field, and Darren Perry (39) gets some low-fives from his teammates. Kordell Stewart warms up.

"We have to win this game for me to cut these locks—that's the way I look at it. My wife is going to be ready. I think she is going to have the scissors here at the stadium so she can run onto the field and start chopping."

—*Kevin Greene, Pittsburgh*

"I'm not going to lie to you: My heart is with the Steelers."

—*Terry Bradshaw, retaining a rooting right despite a much-publicized unhappy parting with the Pittsburgh franchise. Bradshaw did not attend the game.*

Former Super Bowl MVPs Marcus Allen and Steve Young were on hand, as were most of the MVPs from past Super Bowls.

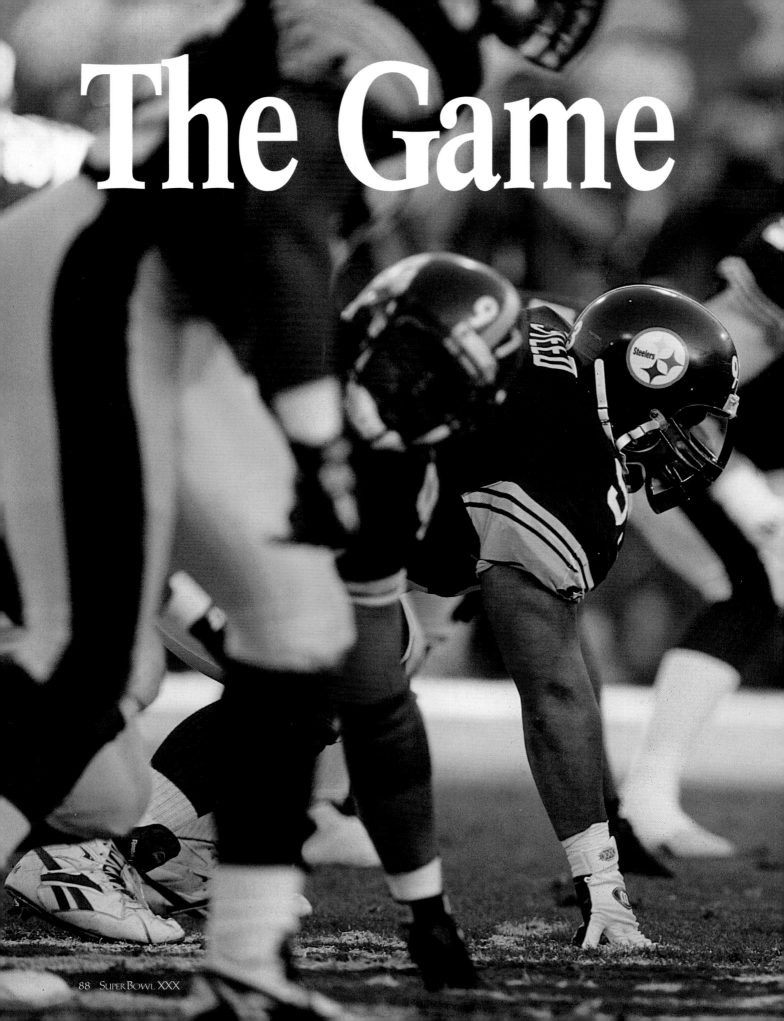

The Game

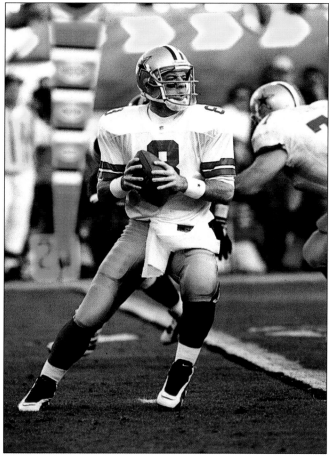

"I think that they are the best team we have played this year."
—*Barry Switzer, Dallas*

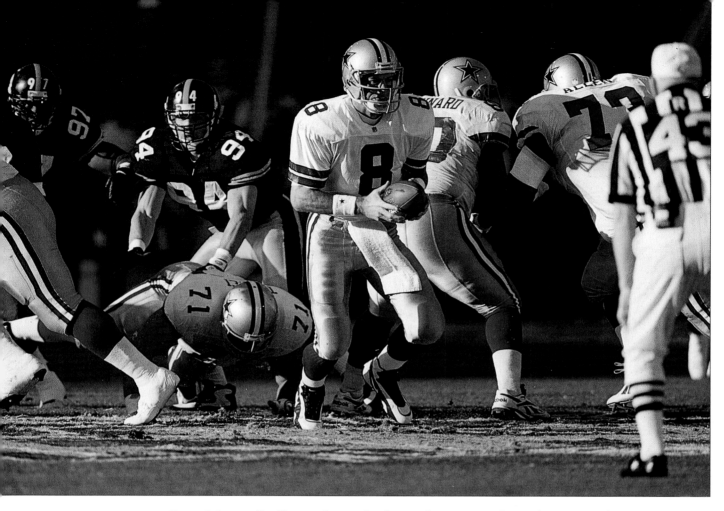

Norm Johnson finally puts foot to leather as the pre-game hype of Super Bowl XXX gives way to the action on the field. Dallas came out gunning with Troy Aikman hitting Michael Irvin with a 20-yard completion on the second play from scrimmage.

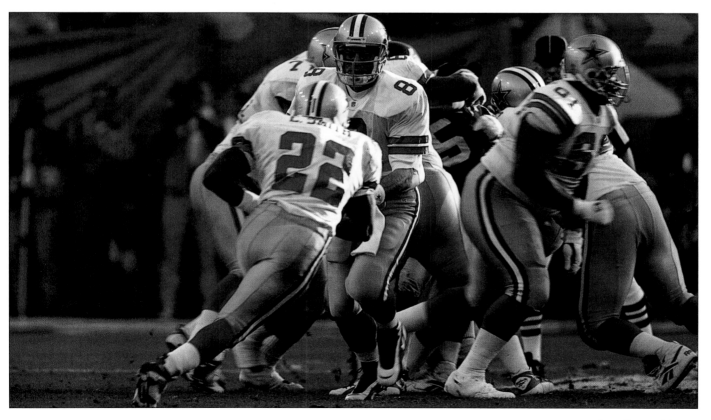

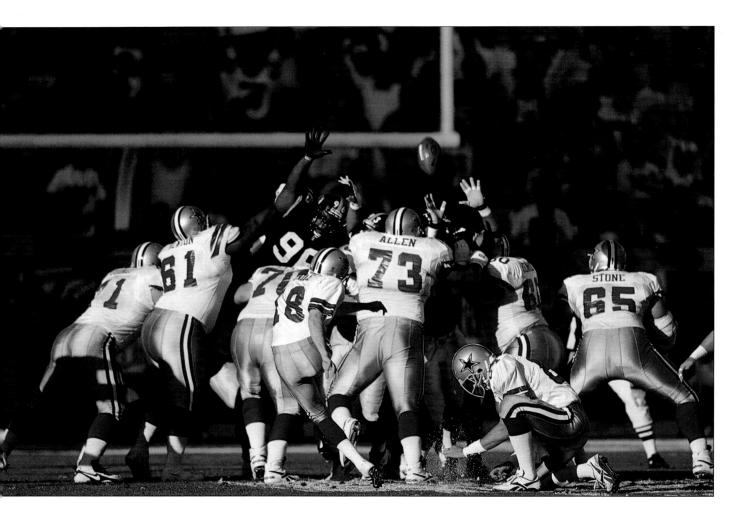

Clockwise from top, the Cowboys drove to the Pittsburgh 24 before Chris Boniol kicked them into an early 3-0 lead; Erric Pegram searches for daylight; Neil O'Donnell throws to Andre Hastings.

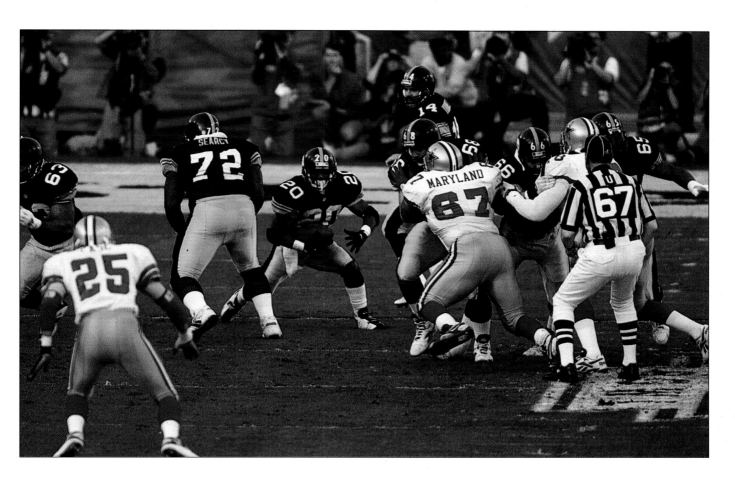

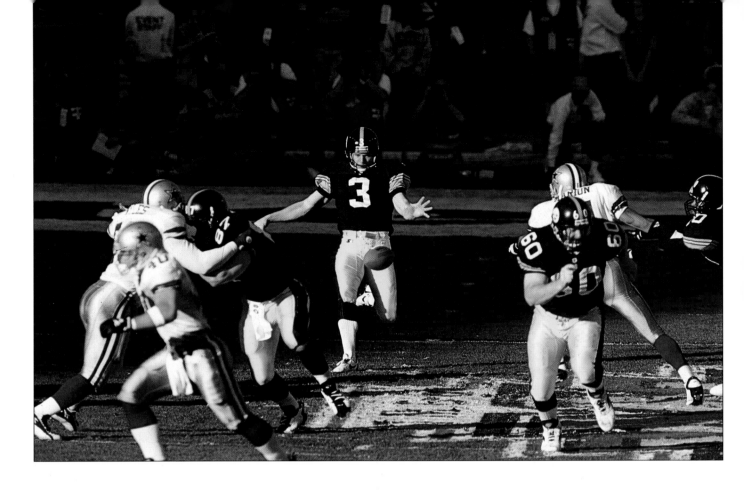

Clockwise from top, Rohn Stark punts; Emmitt Smith is brought down by Levon Kirkland and Greg Lloyd; as the Cowboys march down the field, Deion Sanders hauls in a 47-yard pass from Troy Aikman; Neil O'Donnell spins away from center.

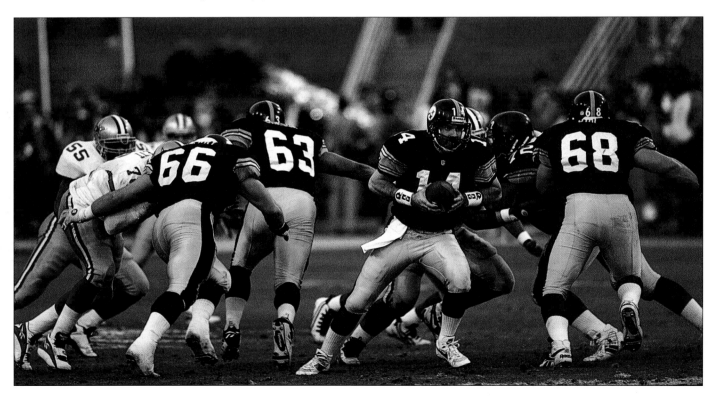

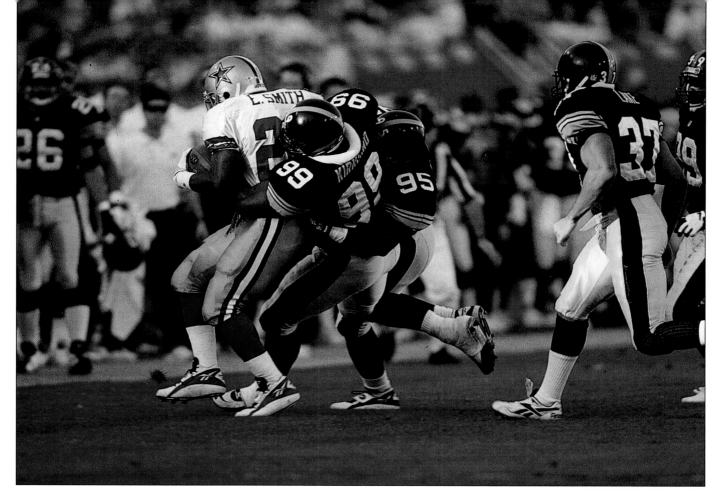

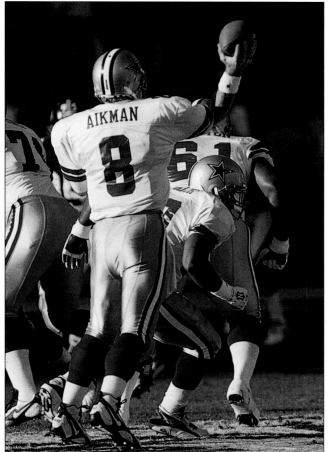

"Our offensive line means a great deal to me. Not only to me, but to this whole team. As they go, we go."

—*Emmitt Smith, Dallas*

Jay Novacek takes Troy Aikman's 3-yard pass for a touchdown and a 10-0 Dallas lead. Though still early in the game, the Steelers knew that a large deficit would be tough to overcome against Dallas, and Bill Cowher offered advice to the troops on the sideline.

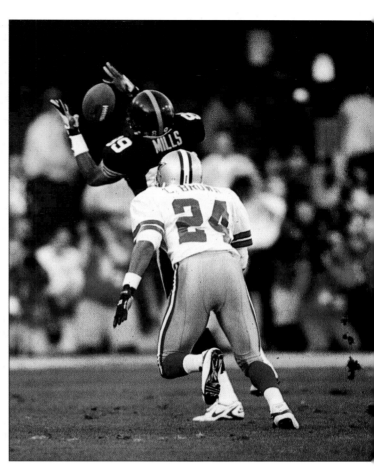

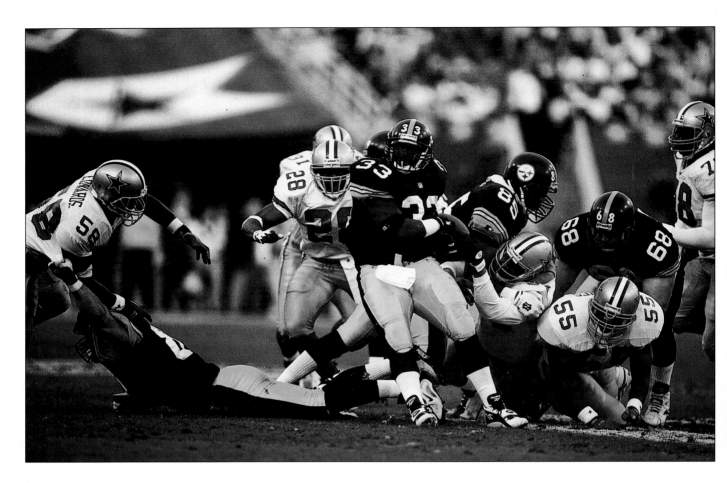

Above and left, Bam Morris and Kordell Stewart tried to spark the Steelers, but Pittsburgh ended the first quarter scoreless. Right, Jay Novacek (84) and Michael Irvin moved Dallas into scoring position once again early in the second quarter.

"Ever since I first stepped in with the Cowboys, it's been a lot of fun having a quarterback like Troy—the best quarterback there is in the NFL. Troy's the one who makes us."

—Jay Novacek,
Dallas

"I remember my father said, 'Mike, if you don't want to go to school, that's fine, you can come out and work on the roof.' I said okay, I don't want to go to school. So I went out on the roof for a couple of days. I said, 'Dad, I want to go to school. I want to be a scholar.' That was tough work."

—*Michael Irvin, Dallas*

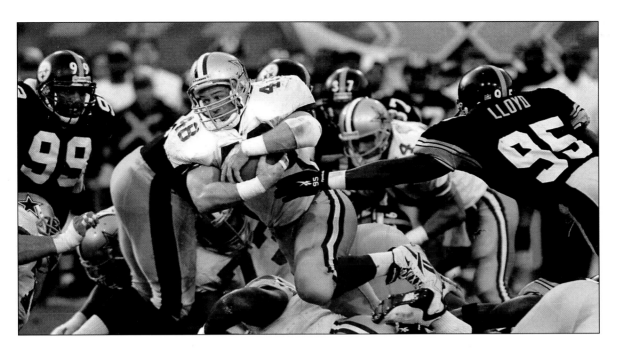

Dallas missed a golden opportunity to open up a huge lead when Michael Irvin's 24-yard touchdown (top) catch was nullified by his offensive pass interference penalty. Dallas was forced to settle for another Chris Boniol field goal and a 13-0 lead.

"Once you get there, there is no stopping. There is no happiness anywhere short of the Super Bowl."

—*Michael Irvin, Dallas*

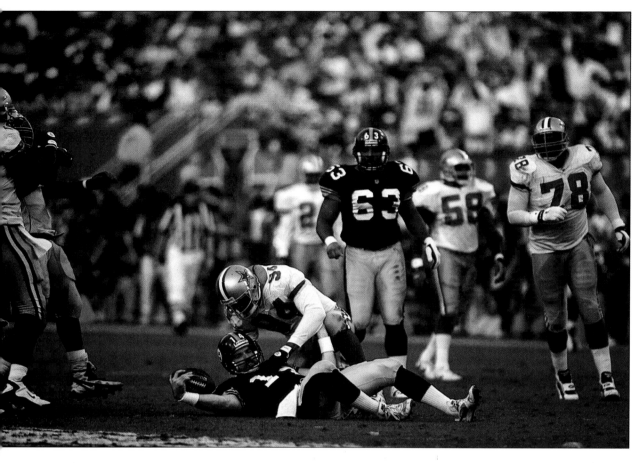

"I felt going in at halftime, we were just getting warmed up. We had just gotten the kinks out— the jitters, whatever you want to call them."

—Rod Woodson, Pittsburgh

Despite a back problem that sidelined him for much of the regular season and playoffs, Charles Haley, above, made his presence felt. Neil O'Donnell, above right, spins to hand off, while Yancey Thigpen gives the Steelers their first score just before the half.

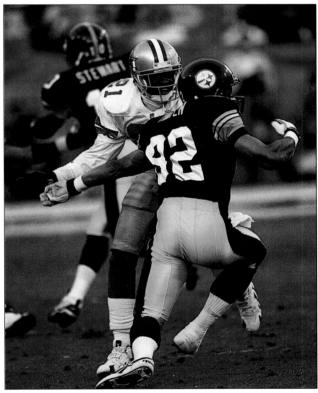

"There is a lot of tradition with the Steelers, but we've got something going for ourselves that is unique."
  —*Kevin Greene, Pittsburgh*

With the score 13-7 at the half, Cowboys Coach Barry Switzer and Larry Allen (73) know that their team could easily be ahead by a lot more than 13-7.

"I'm a working man's man because I work hard for everything I have. Don't let all this [clothes and jewelry] fool you."

—*Deion Sanders, Dallas*

Diana Ross provides the musical backbeat and the dazzling costumes to the halftime pyrotechnics in the desert. Her performance, a montage of her greatest hits, was punctuated by her departure via helicopter.

The second half starts with the same pattern as the first half: both teams use their powerful backs—Bam Morris, below, and Emmitt Smith, below right—with a sprinkling of passes, to control the ball.

"What I do is sack the quarterback. That's what they pay me to do. It's a good feeling. It's an ecstatic feeling. It relieves a lot of stress because I put a lot of pressure on myself to be productive."

—*Kevin Greene, Pittsburgh*

"The first [interception] was big, but Pittsburgh was able to fight back. I think the second one took a lot out of them because our offense pushed it right in and didn't give them much time to do anything."
—*Larry Brown, Dallas*

The first of Larry Brown's two interceptions gave Dallas the ball on Pittsburgh's 18-yard line.

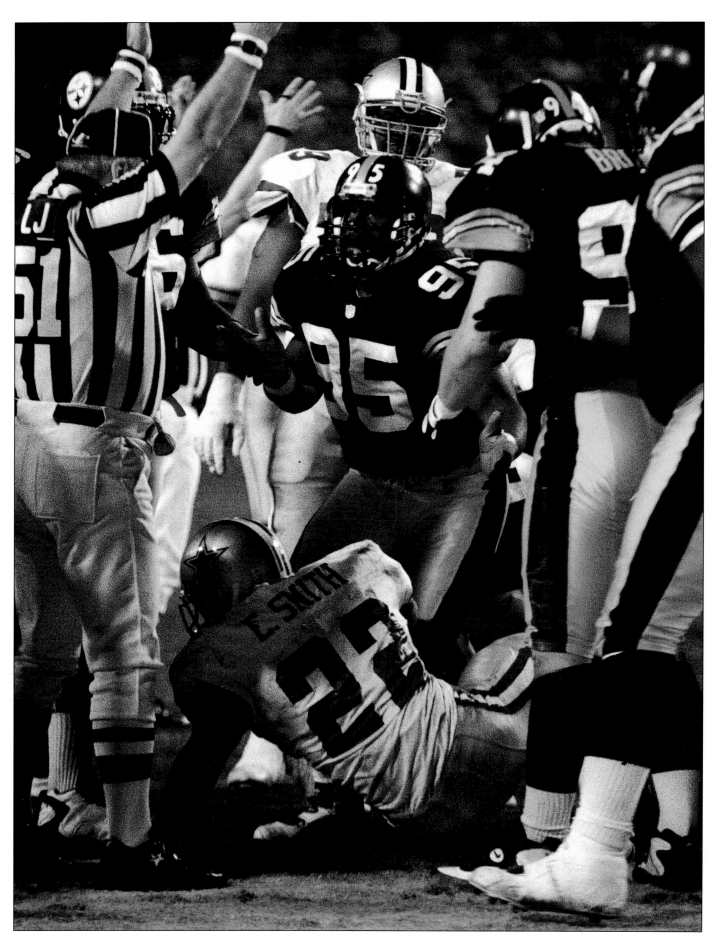

After Larry Bown's first interception gave the Cowboys a first down on Pittsburgh's 18, Troy Aikman hit Michael Irvin for a first down on the 1, then Emmitt Smith scored on the next play to put the Cowboys up 20-7.

"I thought my offensive line played extremely well. Those guys stayed in there and blocked some tough rushers, Leon Lett, all those guys, so I tip my hat to them. They've been good to me all year, they've protected me all year."
—Neil O'Donnell, Pittsburgh

"I definitely think we got the respect
of the Dallas Cowboys today."
—*Darren Perry, Pittsburgh*

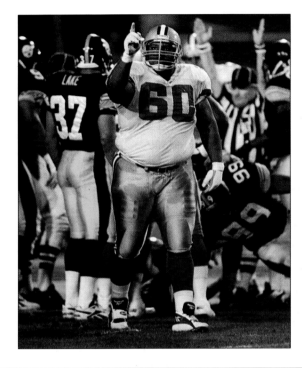

*Opposite, John L. Williams runs to the right
side. Clockwise from top left, Cowboy center
Derek Kennard; O'Donnell is sacked by Chad
Hennings; Pittsburgh's Ernie Mills; the
Cowboys' Larry Allen.*

"As we were walking off the field, I told Neil O'Donnell to look at the big picture, not just this game. We wouldn't have been here without him. It's disappointing to come this far and see how this thing materialized, but we had a great run."

—*Bill Cowher, Pittsburgh*

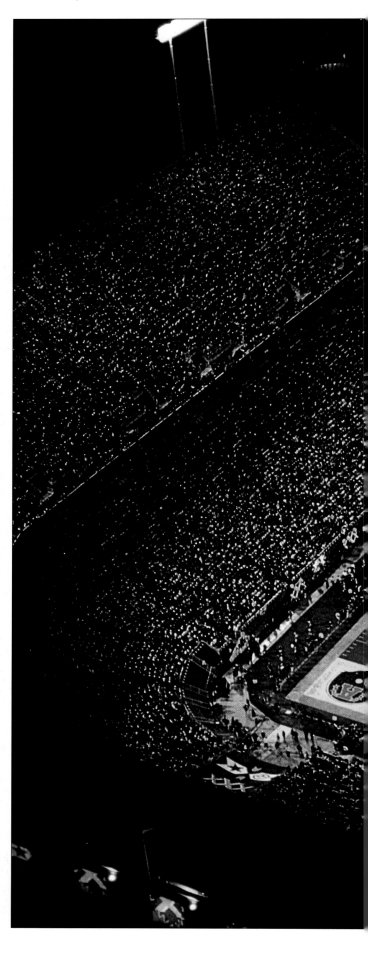

Playing in his first game since knee surgery in early September, Rod Woodson, opposite, breaks up this pass to Michael Irvin late in the third quarter, forcing a Cowboys punt.

Below, Ernie Mills had eight catches for the day. Opposite top, John L. Williams cuts outside to avoid a tackle. Opposite below, this sack of Neil O'Donnell was followed by Norm Johnson's field goal, cutting the Cowboys' lead to 20-10. Trailing by 10 with 11:20 to go, the Steelers needed a big play . . . and they got it on the ensuing kickoff.

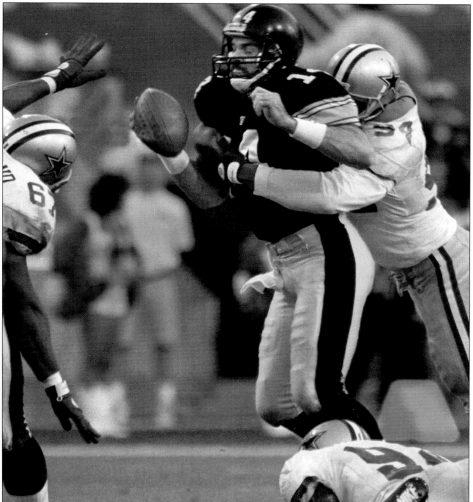

"Every time Troy Aikman throws the ball it's always a perfect throw. That's hard to get from any other quarterback."

—*Jay Novacek, Dallas*

In one of the boldest calls in Super Bowl history, the Steelers, trailing 20-10, tried an onside kick following their field goal. The Cowboys never saw it coming, and the Steelers' Deon Figures, above and right, recovered the ball on Pittsburgh's 48. This led to a Bam Morris 1-yard touchdown run, below, that cut the lead to just three points. Opposite, Levon Kirkland (99) sacks Troy Aikman, helping to give the ball back to Pittsburgh. But hopes of a comeback were deflated on Pittsburgh's next possession. O'Donnell was again intercepted by Larry Brown, far right, and two plays later Emmitt Smith scored for a 27-17 lead, effectively ending Super Bowl XXX.

"I think we felt the game slipping away a little bit after the onside kick."
—*Troy Aikman, Dallas*

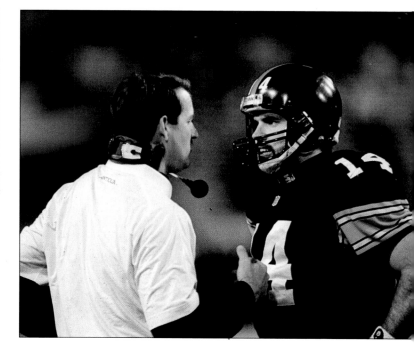

Clockwise from top left, as time winds down, Erik Williams begins to celebrate; Emmitt Smith accepts congratulations; Bill Cowher and the Steelers are left to contemplate what might have been; Charles Haley displays the five fingers upon which his five Super Bowl rings will rest; Emmitt Smith lets his happiness show; Brock Marion intercepts Neil O'Donnell's last throw of the day.

"When we were leading 20-17, I just thought, 'We need a touchdown.' That's all. And let me tell you something, I never at one point doubted we could do it. That's the truth."

—*Michael Irvin, Dallas*

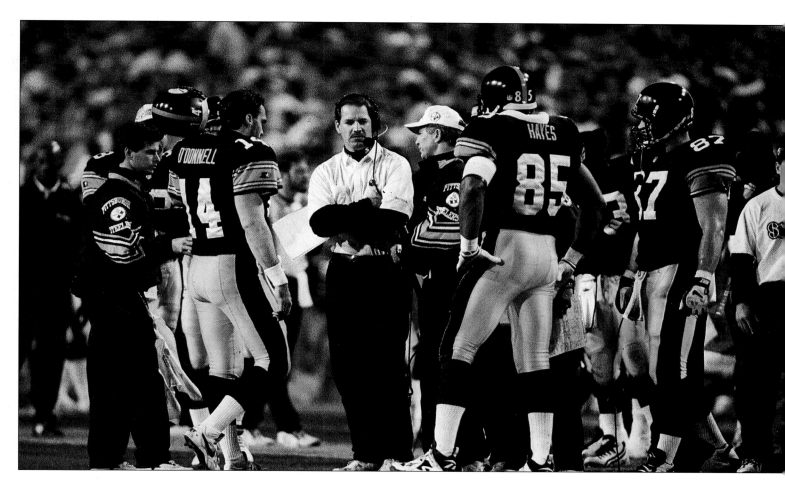

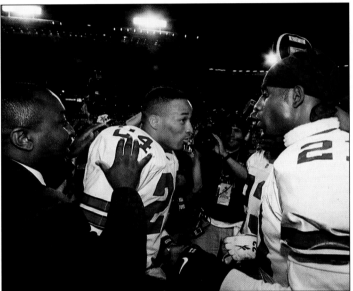

Emotions bubble to the surface, both in joy and in sorrow. Clockwise from left, Deion Sanders and Larry Brown bask in the glow of victory; Barry Switzer hugs the game's MVP; Brentson Buckner sits dejectedly; Pittsburgh fans echo the team's mood; Mark Bruener (87) and Eric Bjornson walk off together; though saddened by the loss, the Steelers know that they had a great season; Greg Lloyd sits alone.

"Don't close the book, it's not the last chapter, we've still got chapters to write."
—*Michael Irvin, Dallas*

Clockwise from top left, Larry Brown leaves the field; George Hegamin sums up the mood of the Cowboys; Troy Aikman wades through the masses; Bill Bates celebrates.

Aftermath

"I feel like we lost the game. We definitely lost the game. You can't come out and have two turnovers and expect to win the Super Bowl."
—*Carnell Lake,*
Pittsburgh

Top and bottom left, Jerry Jones and Barry Switzer hold the ultimate prize: the Vince Lombardi Trophy; Deion Sanders wades through the crowd holding the trophy.

Clockwise from above, Cowboys' Owner Jerry Jones; the celebration goes on; Commissioner Paul Tagliabue presents Larry Brown with the MVP Trophy; Larry Brown, Greg Gumbel (NBC)Michael Irvin & Emmitt Smith; Troy Aikman.

Below, Barry Switzer and Jerry Jones listen to Larry Brown as he speaks with President Clinton; bottom, Deion Sanders addresses the media.

"All week long, they said we were in limos. Sure, we were in limos. We're stars. How else is a star supposed to travel?"

—*Deion Sanders, Dallas*

Below, Jerry and Gene Jones. Players enjoying the victory parade in Dallas include, left to right, Charlie Williams and Greg Briggs; Larry Brown, Darrin Smith and Billy Davis; Michael Irvin.

Appendix

Super Bowl XXX
Sun Devil Stadium
January 28, 1996

Dallas Cowboys	10	3	7	7—27
Pittsburgh Steelers	0	7	0	10—17

Attendance: 76,347   Time of Game: 3:24

Officials
Referee:	Red Cashion (43)
Line Judge:	Dale Orem (51)
Head Linesman:	Paul Weidner (87)
Field Judge:	Don Hakes (96)
Umpire:	John Keck (67)
Side Judge	Bill Carollo (63)
Back Judge	Dick Creed (61)

Scoring Plays

Cowboys, First Quarter, 12:05: Chris Boniol kicks a 42-yard field goal. Scoring drive: 7 plays, 47 yards, 2:55.

Cowboys, First Quarter, 5:23: Jay Novacek scores on a 3-yard pass from Troy Aikman. Chris Boniol kicks the extra point. Scoring drive: 8 plays, 75 yards, 4:35.

Cowboys, Second Quarter, 6:03: Chris Boniol kicks a 35-yard field goal. Scoring drive: 14 plays, 62 yards, 8:44.

Steelers, Second Quarter, 0:13: Yancey Thigpen scores on a 6-yard pass from Neil O'Donnell. Norm Johnson kicks the extra point. Scoring drive: 13 plays, 54 yards, 3:39.

Cowboys, Third Quarter, 6:42: Emmitt Smith scores on a 1-yard run. Chris Boniol kicks the extra point. Scoring drive: 2 plays, 18 yards, 0:36.

Steelers, Fourth Quarter, 11:20: Norm Johnson kicks a 46-yard field goal. Scoring drive: 11 plays, 52 yards, 4:44.

Steelers, Fourth Quarter, 6:36: Bam Morris scores on a 1-yard run. Norm Johnson kicks the extra point. Scoring drive, 9 plays, 52 yards, 4:44.

Cowboys, Fourth Quarter, 3:43: Emmitt Smith scores on a 4-yard run. Chris Boniol kicks the extra point. Scoring drive: 2 plays, 6 yards, 0:18.

STARTING LINEUPS

Dallas Cowboys

Offense
No.	Player	Position
85	Kevin Williams	wide receiver
71	Mark Tuinei	left tackle
61	Nate Newton	left guard
60	Derek Kennard	center
73	Larry Allen	right guard
79	Erik Williams	right tackle
84	Jay Novacek	tight end
88	Michael Irvin	wide receiver
8	Troy Aikman	quarterback
22	Emmitt Smith	running back
48	Daryl Johnston	running back

Defense
No.	Player	Position
92	Tony Tolbert	left end
67	Russell Maryland	left tackle
78	Leon Lett	right tackle
94	Charles Haley	right end
58	Dixon Edwards	strongside linebacker
55	Robert Jones	middle linebacker
59	Darrin Smith	weakside linebacker
21	Deion Sanders	left cornerback
24	Larry Brown	right cornerback
28	Darren Woodson	strong safety
31	Brock Marion	free safety

Others
11 Wade Wilson, quarterback; 18 Chris Boniol, kicker; 19 John Jett, punter; 20 Sherman Williams, running back; 23 Robert Bailey, cornerback; 25 Scott Case, safety; 29 Alundis Brice, cornerback; 38 David Lang, running back; 40 Bill Bates, safety; 42 Charlie Williams, safety; 43 Greg Briggs, safety; 52 Jim Schwantz, linebacker; 65 Ron Stone, guard; 69 George Hegamin, tackle; 70 Dale Hellestrae, center; 82 Cory Fleming, wide receiver; 83 Kendell Watkins, tight end; 86 Eric Bjornson, tight end; 87 Billy Davis, wide receiver; 95 Chad Hennings, defensive tackle; 96 Shante Carver, defensive end; 98 Godfrey Myles, linebacker; 99 Hurvin McCormack, defensive end.

Pittsburgh Steelers

Offense
No.	Player	Position
82	Yancey Thigpen	wide receiver
65	John Jackson	left tackle
66	Tom Newberry	left guard
63	Dermontti Dawson	center
68	Brenden Stai	right guard
72	Leon Searcy	right tackle
87	Mark Bruener	tight end
89	Ernie Mills	wide receiver
14	Neil O'Donnell	quarterback
20	Erric Pegram	running back
22	John L. Williams	running back

Defense
No.	Player	Position
96	Brentson Buckner	left end
93	Joel Steed	nose tackle
97	Ray Seals	right end
91	Kevin Greene	left outside linebacker
99	Levon Kirkland	left inside linebacker
94	Chad Brown	right inside linebacker
95	Greg Lloyd	right outside linebacker
27	Willie Williams	left cornerback
37	Carnell Lake	right cornerback
40	Myron Bell	strong safety
39	Darren Perry	free safety

Others
3 Rohn Stark, punter; 9 Norm Johnson, kicker; 10 Kordell Stewart, wide receiver/quarterback; 18 Mike Tomczak, quarterback; 21 Deon Figures, cornerback; 24 Chris Oldham, cornerback; 25 Fred McAfee, running back; 26 Rod Woodson, cornerback; 29 Randy Fuller, cornerback; 33 Byron (Bam) Morris, running back; 34 Tim Lester, running back; 41 Lethon Flowers, safety; 54 Donta Jones, linebacker; 55 Jerry Olsavsky, linebacker; 60 Kendall Gammon, center; 73 Justin Strzelczyk, guard; 76 Kevin Henry, defensive end; 79 James Parrish, tackle; 83 Corey Holliday, wide receiver; 85 Jonathan Hayes, tight end; 88 Andre Hastings, wide receiver; 90 Bill Johnson, nose tackle; 92 Jason Gildon, linebacker.

FINAL TEAM STATISTICS

	Cowboys	Steelers
TOTAL FIRST DOWNS		
by rushing	15	25
by passing	5	9
by penalty	0	1
THIRD DOWN EFFICIENCY	2-10-20%	9-19-47%
FOURTH DOWN EFFICIENCY	1-1-100%	2-4-50%
TOTAL NET YARDS	254	310
Total offensive plays	50	84
Average gain per play	5.1	3.7
NET YARDS RUSHING	56	103
Total rushing plays	25	31
Average gain per rush	2.2	3.3
NET YARDS PASSING	198	207
Sacks-Yards lost	2-11	4-32
PASS ATTEMPTS-COMPLETIONS-INT.	23-15-0	49-28-3
Average gain per attempt	7.9	3.9

KICKOFFS-IN END ZONE-TOUCHBACKS	6-0-0	4-0-0
PUNTS-AVERAGE	5-38.2	4-44.8
PUNT RETURNS-YARDS	1-11	2-18
KICKOFF RETURNS-YARDS	3-37	5-96
INTERCEPTIONS-RETURN YARDS	3-77	0-0
PENALTIES-YARDS	5-25	2-15
FUMBLES-YARDS LOST	0-0	2-0
FIELD GOALS-ATTEMPTS	2-2	1-1
TIME OF POSSESSION	26:11	33:49

RECEIVING
Cowboys: Irvin 5-76; Novacek 5-50; K.Williams 2-29; Sanders 1-47; Johnston 1-4; Smith 1-3. Total: 15-209, 1 TD.
Steelers: Hastings 10-98; Mills 8-78; Thigpen 3-19; Morris 3-18; Holliday 2-19; J.Williams 2-7. Total: 28-239, 1 TD.

INTERCEPIONS
Cowboys: L. Brown 2-77; B. Marion 1-0. Total: 3-77
Steelers: None

PUNTING
Cowboys: J. Jett 5-191-38-2
Steelers: R. Stark 4-179-44.8

PUNT RETURNS
Cowboys: D. Sanders 1-11; (1 downed, 2 touchbacks)
Steelers: A. Hastings 2-18; (2 downed, 1 touchback)

KICKOFF RETURNS
Cowboys: K. Williams 2-24; B. Marion 1-13. Total: 3-37
Steelers: E. Mills 4-79; F. McAfee   1-17. Total: 5-96

TACKLES (ASSIST)
Cowboys: Woodson 7 (3); Jones 4 (4); Case 6 (1); Brown 5 (2); Marion 5 (2); Edwards 4 (1); Tolbert 4 (1); Smith 3 (2); Carver 3 (1); Haley 3 (1); Bailey 3 (0); Hennnings 3 (0); Maryland 3 (0); Bates 2 (1); Lett 2 (1); Myles 1 (0); Schwantz 1 (0). Total: 79.
Steelers: Kirkland 8 (2); Lloyd 5 (3); Lake 5 (0); W.Williams 4 (1); Perry 2 (3); Steed 3 (1); Bell 2 (1); Brown 1 (2); Greene 2 (0); Olsavsky 1 (1); Buckner 1 (0); Seals 1 (0). Total: 49.

FINAL INDIVIDUAL STATISTICS
RUSHING
Cowboys: Smith 18-49; Johnston 2-8; K.Williams 1-2; Aikman 4-(-)3. Total 25-56.
Steelers: Morris 19-73; Pegram 6-15; Stewart 4-15; O'Donnell 1-0; J.Williams 1-0. Total 31-103.

PASSING
Cowboys: Aikman 15-23-0, 209 yards, 1 TD.
Steelers: O'Donnell 28-49-3, 239 yards, 1 TD.

BALL POSSESSION AND DRIVE CHART

DALLAS COWBOYS

No.	Time Recd.	Time Lost	Time Poss.	How Ball Obtained	Drive Bgn.	No. Play	Yds. Gain	Yds. Pen.	Net Yds.	1st Down	Last Scrm.	How Given Up
1	15:00	12:05	2:55	Kickoff	DC29	7	47	0	47	2	PS24	Field Goal
2	9:58	5:23	4:35	Punt	DC25	8	80	-5	75	4	PS3	TD
3	14:47	6:03	8:44	Punt	DC20	14	67	-5	62	4	PS18	Field Goal
4	4:56	3:52	1:04	Punt	DC14	3	0	0	0	0	DC14	Punt
5	0:13	0:00	0:13	Kickoff	DC38	1	-1	0	-1	0	DC38	Half
				H A L F T I M E								
6	12:07	9:14	2:53	Punt	DC20	5	18	0	18	1	DC38	Punt
7	7:18	6:42	0:36	Intercept	PS18	2	18	0	18	2	PS1	TD
8	1:26	0:33	0:53	Downs	PS47	3	6	0	6	0	PS41	Punt
9	6:36	4:15	2:21	Kickoff	DC12	4	15	0	15	1	DC27	Punt
10	4:01	3:43	0:18	Intercept	PS6	2	6	0	6	1	PS4	TD
11	1:42	0:03	1:39	Downs	DC40	3	-2	-5	-7	0	DC33	Punt

PITTSBURGH STEELERS

No.	Time Recd.	Time Lost	Time Poss.	How Ball Obtained	Drive Bgn.	No. Play	Yds. Gain	Yds. Pen.	Net Yds.	1st Down	Last Scrm.	How Given Up
1	12:05	9:58	2:07	Kickoff	PS25	3	9	0	9	0	PS34	Punt
2	5:23	14:47	5:36	Kickoff	PS27	13	34	0	34	3	DC39	Punt
3	6:03	4:56	1:07	Kickoff	PS32	3	-1	0	-1	0	PS31	Punt
4	3:52	0:13	3:39	Punt	PS46	13	54	0	54	5	DC6	TD
				H A L F T I M E								
5	15:00	12:07	2:53	Kickoff	PS40	6	27	0	27	2	DC33	Punt
6	9:14	7:18	1:56	Punt	PS36	5	12	0	12	1	PS48	Intercept
7	6:42	1:26	5:16	Kickoff	PS15	10	32	0	32	2	PS47	Downs
8	0:33	11:20	4:13	Punt	PS20	11	52	0	52	4	DC28	Field Goal
9	11:20	6:36	4:44	kickoff	PS48	9	52	0	52	5	DC1	TD
10	4:15	4:01	0:14	Punt	PS32	2	0	0	0	0	PS32	Intercept
11	3:43	1:41	2:01	Kickoff	PS24	9	31	5	36	3	DC40	Downs
12	0:03	0:00	0:03	Punt	PS42	1	0	0	0	0	PS42	Intercept

Time of Possession by Quarter	1ST	2ND	3RD	4TH	TOTAL
Dallas Cowboys	7:30	10:01	4:22	4:18	26:11
Pittsburgh Steelers	7:30	4:59	10:38	10:42	33:49

Kickoff Drive No.-Start Average   Cowboys: 3-DC26   Steelers 7-PS30

The Publisher wishes to thank the following companies for their support:

𝕻ittsburgh 𝕻ost-𝕲azette

Indian River Sports Travel
KVIL-FM
The Daily Oklahoman
The Vindicator
Tribune Newspapers
Westcor Shopping Centers
Wheaties
Zenith Data Systems

McCOMBS CLASSIC HENDRIX
AUSTIN   ROUNDROCK   AUSTIN
THE STRENGTH OF EXPERIENCE

Red McCombs GMC Truck
Classic GMC Truck
Hendrix GMC Truck

WOODFORD PUBLISHING, INC.
660 Market Street, Suite 206
San Francisco, CA 94104
(415) 397-1853

Laurence J. Hyman
Publisher and Creative Director

Jim Santore
Art Director

David Lilienstein
Vice President Marketing & Development

Rob Kelly
Editor

Tony Khing
Director of Advertising

Heather Torain
Assistant Editor

Paul Durham
Debbie Fong
Wendy Gardner
Marketing Assistants

To order
THE OFFICIAL BOOK OF
SUPER BOWL XXX:
Showdown in the Desert,
please call 1-800-359-3373

To order the original 9-1/2" x 48"
panoramic photograph on pages 58-59,
contact LaPayne Photography at
800-280-8994.

PHOTOGRAPHY CREDITS

Tony Bennett: 140A; 141A
Dennis Desprois: Back CoverTR; 1; 16-17; 18; 19A, 20BR; 20-21T; 21A; 22; 45TR; 53TR; 83B; 96BR; 97TL; 106; 107A; 120BR; 131TR
Beth Hansen: 23A; 36-37; 46T; 48T; 50-51A; 55T & B; 57B; 64-65; 67A; 68-69T; 69TR; 74T; 78BL; 79BL; 92B; 138T & BR
Brad LaPayne: 58-59
David Lilienstein: 4-5; 20BL; 40 BL & R; 41A; 42A; 47B; 52T; 66B; 68BL; 68-69B; 78MR; 82TL; 109T; 110TL & LTM; 139T
Baron Wolman: Front Cover; 38-39T; 70-71; 72T; 108; 122-123

NFL Photographers:
Courtesy NFL: 8L, BR; 9; 10A; 11; 12; 13; 14A; 15A
John E. Biever: 9; 10T
Peter Brouillet: Back CoverM; 2-3; 47T; 48BL; 49T; 52BL & BR; 54B; 75TR; 79T; 80B; 90BL; 92T; 97TR; 100BL; 114; 115TR; 116; 120TR; 128TL

Dave Cross: 6-7
Malcolm W. Emmons: 10B
Gerald Gallegos: 35; 38BL; 40T; 44A & R; 45B; 56B; 75TL; 115B; 120BL; 127BR; 134-135; 138MR
Ross Lewis: 15T
Al Messerschmidt: Back CoverTL & BL; 6; 14TR; 15B; 24-25A; 25TR; 26A; 28T; 32A; 44-45T; 46B; 49B; 53TL; 57T; 74B; 75B; 76B; 77BL; 78T & LM; 82TR; 83T; 86; 105BR; 110LBM, BL & R; 111; 112-113T; 119B; 125T; 129T; 130TL; 133T; 137T
Mike Moore: 54-55T; 109B; 122L; 133B
Joe Patronite: 73B; 84-85B; 85T; 95T; 99B; 103T; 118
Dick Raphael: 8BL
Bob Rosato: 27; 28BL & BR; 29B; 30T; 31T & BR; 34A; 72B; 77T; 78BR; 79BR; 80BR; 81TR, BL & BR; 82B; 87; 88-89; 93B; 98T; 112B; 113B; 119T; 130LM; 138BL; 139B
G. B. Rose: 73T; 76T; 82 ML; 84T; 96BL; 97B; 105T; 115ML; 117T; 128BR; 129B; 132B
Manny Rubio: 94A; 102B
Paul Spinelli: 29T; 31BL; 38-39B; 53B; 69BR;

138ML; 53B; 69BR
Kevin Terrell: 30B; 33; 80-81T; 90T & BL; 100BR; 102-103T; 103B; 104B; 105BL; 115TL; 131B; 137B
Tony Tomsic: 11; 13; 99T; 104T; 126TR; 136T
Ron Vesely: 43A; 91T; 120TL; 124; 126TL & BL; 128BR
Michael Zagaris: 62; 85R; 95BL; 105BL; 121; 127BL

**The following photographs are
© Pittsburgh Post-Gazette:**
John Beale: 63; 77BR; 90BR; 101T; 132T
Peter Diana: 117BR; 127TR; 128TR
Bob Donaldson: 101B; 102BR; 117BL; 126BR; 127TL; 128BL;
Robin Rombach: 39R; 56T; 60T; 60B; 61; 95BR; 125B; 136B
Darrell Sapp: 66TR
Bill Wade: 48BR; 66TL; 96T; 98T; 100T; 131TL; 130R; 130B

KEY: T=Top; B=Bottom; L=Left; R=Right; M=Middle; A=All